JERSEY MERCY

Other books by Laura McCullough

Poetry
Rigger Death & Hoist Another
Panic
Speech Acts
What Men Want
The Dancing Bear

Anthologies
A Sense of Regard: Essays on Poetry and Race
The Room and the World: Essays on the poet Stephen Dunn

JERSEY MERCY

LAURA MCCULLOUGH

Black
Lawrence
Press

Black
Lawrence
Press

www.blacklawrence.com

Executive Editor: Diane Goettel
Book and cover design: Amy Freels

Copyright © 2016 Laura McCullough
ISBN: 978-1-62557-956-0

Published 2016 by Black Lawrence Press.
Printed in the United States.

Dedicated to my aunt Judy Hardman,
the Wilson Family: cousin Stephanie and her daughters,
Geneva and Vanessa,
and to my mentor and friend, poet Stephen Dunn.

A portion of the proceeds from this book will go to
The Light of Day Foundation.
lightofday.org

Contents

Part III
Horses & Other Beings

Part IV
Funtown

often I cannot tell good fortune from bad
—Robert Pinsky

The boardwalk was where all of New Jersey came together,
where New Jersey, for better or worse, met itself.
—Junot Diaz

Part I

Jersey Mercy

Godstomp Glomp

Didn't hear the stories at the Comix shop, didn't know
he'd tossed time in front of that train, last text was *Glomp*
his friend saying, *The shizzle.* It went down just like that.
Here, then not. I saw my boys after that. All I could do
not to sob against their broken, tatted chests. *Just us,*
is what I wanted to say. What can I trade to make such
things impossible?

Did I tell you today your eyes are beautiful?
How sad they make me, but so glad? How on the train home,
stopped to let another one pass, out my window I saw
on the rocks, a skeleton, large, searing white in the yellow,
September sun? How by the time I got my phone out,
we'd begun to move, the chance to save something lost?

Moon Croon in Eatontown

Mercy and Fred stand spitting seeds outside the porta potty
between the construction site and convenience store;
Rick is inside puking. He's got too much something and not
enough something else—food; restraint; who knows?
Mercy's social is tattooed across her neck. *In case they find
my body,* she told her mother. Now, she sings "Love Me
Tender." Fred is listening past her voice for the next train
to the City, the one so many boys have been jumping in
front of. How many in this handful of years? Some fathers,
too, whose shame has grown on the tracks, and Fred
thinks the whole town is down and afraid. He wants
out. The nighttime whistle seems low and sad; for some
it rings hope, others anger. The train comes this way, goes
that, but everyone ends up in the same place—fly away
or lay down flat—someone singing old Elvis tunelessly
waiting out the night in a 7-Eleven parking lot.

Mercy Gets Her Krump On in Atlantic City and Shows Some Boys How to Dance Like a Girl

Tommy 2 AC Clown pops his ass down
on the boards says, *Show me what you got.*
Mercy says, *You think you know,*
then does her show, going
   diss and sick: bully, beasty, cocky.
All flash, no goof, not yet;
Mid East pop in her iPod, power jerks and rugged,
she mugs a face, has learned grace is thought
weak, ends in pose, says, *You so white,*
without irony, wishing she weren't.

She is grimy and sweaty from her
   snaking and shaking and quaking and twerking,
feeling free right now from fear,
loving to be near what makes her feel alive.

When she gets the bus home, the mile markers
on the Garden State Parkway clicking by
out her window look like the ruler
she will refuse to be beaten with, and she'll calculate
the days until she can go again to,
Show them how it's done.

God's Got Gaming Sense:
Everyone Loves a Slurpee

At the 7-Eleven, the concrete gum pocked and greasy,
the white posts knocked by bumpers and burn marks.
There she is.   Mercy. There he is. Her friend Fred.

He looks good, dressed and fine. Imagines zombies
in the weeds behind them. Their phones ping glory;
they are waiting, once the sun is winked, for what
might happen in the night, this night: cars humming
hope in hot getaways. Someone slurps Slurpee desire:
        mango crush, blue swirl.

Look me in the eye, Mercy says to Fred.
He says, *All I got is what I see.* They love each other in a way,
though he's wearing a skirt. He says, *Zombie's gonna get me.*
Mercy gives him her red lipstick, smiles. They both think
power is in that purse. He turns the tube—talismanic ruby-
red—swipes, blots on a hoagie wrapper. The lights are coming
on yellow as the sky goes gray and blue-black. The ocean
is just a few blocks away, but the train track is out back.

A car pulls up. Mercy gets in. *You look good, Fred*, she yells
as Rick backs out, the windshield glimmering, Fred's image
playing across it like a video in which he is the lone star.

Change the Game

Mercy and Rick play games, are Master Meatsmackers
in the *Kingdom of Loathing*, searching
for their familiars, iced white Canadians
in hands bricked with splints; already
their wrists are shot, but they don't know it.
I think of them as they sit in their screens' glow,
what might be coming. *Lux,* Latin for light—not
from the screens, but what they seek in each other.

Hey, Skullhead, they croak, push glasses
up their nose bridges. Oh, they are so lovely!
Caterpillar brows, off-the-grid Free People shirts,
mismatched Hush Puppies, and argyle knee socks.
What decade is it now? they ask each other,
laughing, when Mercy's mother comes home
tired from work, all out of parenting. When
she slaps Mercy, no one is surprised.

Mercy: Rivet Girl Listen To—

Once, it was other music like a train
out of town. I was that girl. Next door,
it's aggrotech, dubstep, moombahton, power noise.
Grind and krump, Mercy learned to bump
on her front porch. She tells me she likes
          techno, drum and bass, trap, and acid trance.

She says she dreams in dayglo and of Tomorrowland,
but can't get a ticket. I hear her now:
Mom, please send me to Belgium and I swear…

Mom breathes in a whoop; doesn't like Skrillex or Krewella,
wants to keep Rivet Girl at home.   So would I.
Mom sits on their porch, not quite a glamour shot,
looking at the moon, head wreathed
from her Marlboro,
one hand to chest,
trying to breathe.

Say It isn't So, Ho

Her mother yells, *Whore*, and I can hear their fight next door.
What dream-snake will keep Mercy awake as the baby
bumps her ribs? She doesn't think she's the fool
her mother calls her. There's been trouble, double what she
dreamed.   Mother and daughter.   *You can't teach
her nothing*, her mother tells me at the fence. *Please try*,
she asks, but what can I say? *What about your doctor,
teacher, priest?* I suggest. *There's nothing to be lost.*

Mercy may need bed rest, she tells me the next day, but it may
or may not work, and she needs health bennies. *Mom's job
doesn't have any. The baby is due soon. Where is the daddy?*
I ask. Mercy has held fast to silence, told her mother nothing.
Atlantic City, Mercy tells me, *playing poker*; risking it all,
hoping to win. *He's a pro*, Mercy says, patting the belly
no longer a secret. She looks so happy, radiant even,
the beautiful lead in an underfunded, undirected film.

Brainspin Me Another Wunna Those

Poke broke, not filling the tank
because spring might spring
and not enough money for the long winter,
using empty socket, to recharge.
Guy at coffee shop tells Mercy, *Don't plug into my electric.*
She says, *Buy me some sparkle, rub me the right way,*
dancey dance, in your fancy pants.
He can't say anything back, just mugs a face,
mirroring sad and sweet, but thumbs toward the door,
meaning:

Time to leave. Later, at the Monmouth Mall, a girl
who used to be her friend sees her, says, *Got you*
some fabulous on, those chocolate high-tops,
rehab the Starbucks, might even get you a job.

Mercy tells her about the bump.
Oh, no, no—wave of hands—*Pregnant?*
Don't think about it. Somebody got your back,
but next time, check your vag first, 'cause
when you fat, can't fill the tank;
old joke, one way to keep you broke.

Daddy Trance

His brother gives him money for a tat,
says, *Nothing's sacred anymore, Little Bro.*
What he doesn't say is: *The body is so fragile*
   always was, always was; sometimes
   one look is all it takes, a touch, stroke
   of chord, dissonant and true,
   and the bones shift like someone punched you.

Rick wants to be better, doesn't know how.
For big brother. For her. For that baby
they made, someone says is his.

Whatever it takes, he thinks, *whatever,*
but he's caught between two things, can't decide
how to proceed, gets two tats instead:
   Lux and *Cyborg,* one on each bicep,
fills his sleeves; nothing's sacred: between
the fingers and toes, vines curl and weave;
he says, *They're like notes to that song*
always playing in my head. Now
backs of calves are all that's left,
thinks, *Baby names?* But can't imagine
what that means.

Dr. Valentine Blows a Curse (YOLO)

One spring break down in the *Rica*, Rick
got *Live Fast, Die Young* on the backs of his calves.
Now they read: *Live Fast, Die ~~Young~~ Last*
because Mercy's got a baby. But it's not trending,
and baby is metaphor for mutual. Their mothers
say they're about to know what the real deal is,
tilt their heads toward each other like new friends.
Still, Rick is going back to college out of state,
and Mercy's staying local; she's not so vocal
about what she feels, but her body's changed
and changing. She'd like to go to college, too,
wishes she could go somewhere hot in winter,
but for now she just wishes she were thinner,
and that the baby on her hip would sleep.

First to Go, Last to Know

Soldier Boy was his friend: he goes, he comes,
he goes, he went again; was that him they flew
outta that place then?   Hot.   Shot to the head
if sights set, but they got him out before revenge.
What he did, man, can you get behind that?
Text went viral. Some said, *Yeah,* little Hitlers
crying, their world so small, *smack-jab,* easier
than thinking, but did you think anything
would be different:

you can dream *lux* and jade,   clean
on holy day, watch massacre on Monday, and view
them on your way to work. Walk in the door,
see:
            the boy filling the snack machine,
            another dragging in the water bottles,
            sloshing universe of nothing, dreaming of
            digging   that hole
            out on the lawn,   laying wire;
            at least it has health benefits
            and some honor.

Jersey Shore Boards: Got a dollar, man?

I watch Whiskey Willy wheel the boards
with his friend, Crabdaddy, who, bent backwards,
walks on all fours, hence the name.
He's an older guy, never shy, always
talks to you when you pass by, but he smells
of pickles and Pall Malls, so I never answer.

The wind has turned,
coming off the ocean now, and Whiskey Willy
in his manual wheelchair licks the salt off his thin wrist,
small, blue-lined and white, giving off a pale light
as blue dusk begins.

I am listening. Looking in a sideways way.
This isn't my place. He says, *Hey, Crabdaddy,*
what's in the air tonight? Crabdaddy twists around,
his eyes slits, head upside down. *Can't see nothing,*
but something wicked maybe, says he,
Kids coming down, down from all around.
This ain't our space no more. They never look at me.

Whiskey Willy rolls away; Crabdaddy upends
himself, lifts his bucket of change, pulls open
a wide pocket,   pours. He flashes me
a peace sign and a wink. I nod, look
at the water. I can still hear Willy's wheels
clacking
over the wood planks

that don't align anymore.
The new ones are sand-colored, with whirls
of cross grain, smooth. The old ones are cracked,
nails dangerously askew.

Mercy Thinks: the Color of Blood in Any Century

Ai-fans on the boardwalk, Coca-Cola
branded shirts, Ming dynasty vase outline
fades underneath that red and white.
What's read, Wei Wei says, *is what you need
to resist.* Mercy raises her fist; she's lovely
in her dayglo and new tats, never been outside
the state, thinks her fate rests on pop idols
and McDonald's—her first job—all she can get,
licks hot fudge when she refills the machine—
Fuck you, she thinks—uses her tongue, rim
ragged and round, she stays just inside
the metal groove, doesn't make a sound,
looks around; knows some would call this
stealing, but it's sweeter off the jagged lid;
Never been cut, she thinks, *Never will.*

Late Spring, Dignity

Frankie on the boardwalk, skinny
jeans, his head mean, stalks the girl
from his old high school who once
called him a fool. *Here I am again*,
he wants to say, a kind of play that
is no fun, he knows it; if he surprises
her from behind, tatted arm from around,
his hand in her face, would she scream?
Could she ever scream his name?   Mercy

passes

Tino, drumming in his spot—always
Thursday, all-day-late-night across from
The Pony—and she stops, her friends sloppy
next to her. All their hair swaying, wood
heels clacking impatience. Her scrunched
hand from her hip pocket. Dropped coins.
Frankie feels them in his loins. Seagull pecks
his toe, then backs away, wings held high.

In the Air, It's Fair

Nothing seems fair, and soon
forgotten in the flood lights, Stone
Pony, Saturday night, summer,
just off the Asbury boardwalk,
or Philly—weekend, winter—
finding a scene, something less
mean and lonely than her pointless
job nights—Dunkin' Donuts,
midnight shift. The first day,
the boss had looked her up
and down, said, *Size 12*; she
darkened red under her make-up,
double-color hair. *You're so square,*
she'd said, taking the uniform, but
he didn't smile. *Put your hands
in the air*, she yells, circle glow stick
around her neck, pulse quickening
to the music—DJ as artist, named
Somethingthisway—rages as he spins.

Hit the Crash—Symbol

Mercy's left the baby home,
wants to roam like she always tried,
but with no place to go then.
Now anywhere is somewhere
and the boardwalk feels steamy—
clean even in the heat;
the heavy air makes her chest feel full,
wind uplifting the hair from her nape.
Boy playing drums raps a beat, rudiments—
       diddle, flam, drag—
       she recalls from her friend
in band, then drops some change, watches coins
flip from her fingers, the nails all chewed, red-
ragged, like something she can't get over.

The bucket has some singles, and when coins sing,
the drummer hits the crash cymbal,
then the ride, scatters ash from his black
       lung doogie, head spin, hair fly, sweating in the salt air.

Snorkel-fish follies is what he calls girls
like her *what give him dollars and cents*—
thinks, *They only like gents, no rats just fat cats*,
and, *She too pretty*, but, *Her hands look slutty*:
Bottle rat, mouths, *That's okay*.   Bang!
Then sticks on lap, tips his hat,
but she's already gone.

Holy and Crushing

Weatherman say, *Snowpocalypse coming!* Clears
the stores, duct tape running low, lay some up, iced
tea, Twinkies: holy. Make me run, batteries
and cheese, what about some cans? Make them protein,
please. Kids in their beds; sky full of dread. Social

*not*working, neighbors all boxed in. This is *my*
skin you're in. *Sorry, Autotext bopped*
erotic fumble, bobble that snap, snap that
disc; you're out of luck, no scholly for you.

Walk across the street, ring around the moon, some-
thing coming soon, and it's better than you, least
live that way. Neighbor crying on the porch, some-
one died today, see the snow? *Bon hiver, Love,*
Goodbye, and *Snickers are all I got to share.*

Part II

The Depths

The Depths

1.

Almost no light and so cold.

There next to me on the bus, that woman who lives
in the group home who dreams
of angels sleeping
between her teeth. She tells me
they have fallen out.
My babies! She cries, covering her mouth. *I couldn't save them!!*

2.

She said something like that,
the woman at the Goodwill today:
her mother in law dying, then the brother,
then she herself diagnosed with a tumor—
benign, thank god—then her child diagnosed with diabetes,

and her hours cut, so she lost her health benefits,
and all of this just since August,
and the summer now over,
and she never got to the beach this year,
and now winter is coming soon,
and the daylight keeps getting shorter.

3.

No solid surfaces for life to cling to.
No sanctuary, no refuge. Small things
eaten by large because it is not safe to stay

in one place; because creation cannot *not* happen,
nor in one place only; because the weather, wind, and water
collude to make us go—

barracuda; jacks; sailfish; marlin; albacore.

Another name for a pod of sharks = a shiver.

4.

Species intermingled, like Asbury Park,
all that respiration and concrete,
　　　rock formations for people,
　　　hiding in all the crevices,
　　　and much of life simply moderate,
　　　not much doing, equable and even,
　　　the young especially unsatisfied by this,
the far-off dying coral just too far off, a hypothesis at best:

Pierce me; pierce me; let this fierce life take me someplace else.

5.

The bodies of the dead accrue to cities'
formations, millions over millennia;
every hour, every day, some coral polyps
perish and others are born,
those two old stories:
one way in, one way out,
the sea the same, essentially,
and our souls soldered by what?

My Revenant

After the storm, in an old hotel, I opened
the closet door only to find it was not a closet,
but a stairway leading
to a dark basement that was not just an unlit basement,
but one with no light switch or string to pull on,
and I said, *Oh, shit*, because that open-mouthed blackness
swam up at me as if it were a waiting, breathing thing.

Things like this return you to childhood terrors,
your lists of nights
too large to comprehend
that just had to be endured.

I closed that door, locked its little, gold nipple
and turned away, a delicious fear rippling across my shoulders

and asked for another room, one with a shallow closet, shadows
only of an arm's length.   The manager avoided my eyes
when she gave me the new key,   and I wondered
if the barrier between us
was my shame or her guilt,
twin ghosts that never die.

Behind me lay everything
ahead of me.
Ahead of me was everything
to recollect.

What They Thought about the Water

I couldn't leave; who'd tend my birds?   The condition
I'm in is not my fault.   The choices we made to live

here were never sane, but I couldn't drive any more.
          I needed the water even when I felt like a squatter.

The town's falling down.   Oh, it was a flood you say,
and that my dread is overmuch, but it is going to happen

again.   When?   Who knows, but soon and then
          I don't know
what I'll do.   There isn't anyone to sue anymore
          and my insurance
dropped me.   My birds are gone, too. Flew when
          I forgot

to close the cage.   Next time, I'll go, I promise,
couldn't stay   in good conscience,

          like an accomplice
          to my own demise,

unless I get a dog. I might. Help me with the constant fear.
But I am so thin now.   Only yarrow grows
          in my destructed
yard.   And no one has sympathy
          for what happened to me.

Peoples Loves They Animals

A 32.5-foot wave recorded by buoy ten miles out
a record since they started keeping records
makes one wince to think a height so tall might fall
onto a boat a town a house the reason why Sea Bright
had that damned ugly wall 14-foot-high protection
a kind of lie from anything we die—we die from so many things
but don't stop us wanting to live near water local SPCA says
dog got away during storm couldn't find owner
was going to put him down 'til word got around everyone
loves a dog they found the family kids happy living
in a double-the-fee rented place over in Navesink every place
taken and FEMA gonna pay so what could they say
the owners but sure at twice the cost of yesterday
Mr. Marshmallow the dog wasn't allowed but the local paper
took it up so owner had to back down let him stay:

I mean who's gonna pay
landlord told the reporter *if he wrecks the joint*
but what can I do? Everyone
loves a dog.

Out of the Blue, Who

It floated across the sea from Nagasaki, he said,
but wasn't sure a float as massive as a ship sixty
feet or more—a dock most likely, crusted and full
of crabs and snails, sea stars and urchins, sea grasses
and flotation devices, organic looking like a molting
creature—could come ashore from one calamity
to another. *How many birds had rested there,*
took respite from the air? she wondered, the drinks
at Wonder Bar half-priced in the days after the storm,
rotting meat on the streets from restaurant kitchens
emptied and tossed—no public health plan in place
for times like this—and lounge chairs from The Empress
that once impressed and held summer surfers' behinds,
someone sitting on their lap if they were lucky, carousel
twinkling darkly in the dance lights shooting out, beaus
always in the shadows looking for love's stand-in.

Nautical Tattoo

He tells me a turtle once meant a sailor
had passed
the equator; a dragon or swallow or map
of China meant he flew
five thousand miles, and two was double.

A man in trouble might
have a beating held off by a praying Jesus
on his back. If he'd been
to Cape Horn, then stars on his earlobes;
a nautical star,

five pointed and dark, meant to be a psychic
light to guide the sailor
home when lost. Some with angel wings.
A red one and a green one
on the chest was a warning, said, *I am best;*

*give way. Who can wear
a thing like this today,* I ask, my bare arm against
the rest, his pen poised.
Narrative has given way, he says,
but each of us is still the star in the center

of our own universe.
My fingers clench; the muscles in my forearm tense;
I'm posing and know it.
Once a student said I needed a tattoo for the experience
of pain. *That's a country*

we've all been to, I'd said, even then floundering.
What right had I earned
to respond that way? As if I could speak the same
language as him,
as if I actually knew my own way home.

Shot it. It was me. You have to believe it.

They are at the WindMill in Long Branch
ordering burgers at 2 am. *That's not funny,*

Mercy says, but wonders if it's true. Headline
in the local paper says: Beached Whale Shot

thru Blow Hole, Died and Washed Up. *I was
out crabbing with Sammy. Saw this shimmer*

in the water. What I do? he said. *Thought it
was a monster.* She says, *No fool thinks*

such a fool thing. He drinks his drink. *You
saw Jaws,* is all he says. She smirks,

You're such a jerk, says, *Where you get the gun?*
but she doesn't doubt he has one. She grew

up smart, knows $300 gets one off the street,
so he doesn't have to answer. Instead, he

pulls a cigarrette from his breast pocket,
takes it outside. Through the glass she watches

his face, smoke like seaweed swaying rings
around his head; looks like an angel to her—halo

glow—his eyes look weepy, weary, sorry.
His burgers are done; she waves him back in.

Resistance and Surrender

What can I say that won't undermine the truth
of the turtle I sat watching? Waiting for the intermittent blink
of its striped eye, I really wanted it to feel safe
enough to move again, so I could track it back to the sea.
It had dug a nest near the dunes, but laid no eggs.
I was patient. Forty-five minutes I watched,
which is true, but beside the point. Soon enough
it was a dark spot—having given up and crawled to the wrack line,
the dropping waves, too cool for me to enter—
and was gone. Walking to the empty bowl she'd left,
the waves continued to build and fall behind me

and in the air

the sound of music coming from the pier, someone
strumming alone on a guitar, blinking in the wind.

From Whence We Come, We Go

Argo, network of submersible robots,
three feet long, singing their song to the surface
with what we want to know: *How hot? How fast? How long?*
How wrong?   Three thousand
each on a seven-year journey
down and up, sensing, relaying, one voice alone
not enough, together mapping the song of the sea
to us on shore. How salty is the sea today compared
to a decade ago? Argo's data plotted into grids,
so we can absorb and extrapolate.

We cyborgs sit in our office shells, pearls
of wisdom forming from information
we can't collect and still protect ourselves or anything at all.
The sea inside is wide and far from those who sit
next door, but collectively, like a coral reef,
we are asleep and extend the senses toward each other,
all our heads receiving and transponding; down we dive,
some of us returning, like the three thousand, see them surface,
then collected, refurbished (or rejected), then returned.

Glory of the Seas

The puka shell has a hole that is not bored or broken
but found and threaded makes a string worn for luck

or safe voyage, now not common, though still casual,
beads formed from other shells or even plastic. But

the snail that coils inside the shell is as beautiful if not
more so than the shell found on the shore, flesh striated

and luminous, attracting attention, but has venom—small
ones like an insect sting; larger ones can kill—multitude

of compounds, finding ground in medicine, paralyzing
pain better than morphine and non-addicting, a trick then

for the body, without the risk. And the shell, once prized
and expensive, now is not, since we have dived so low

and found where they were hidden, brought them out;
            newly commoditized: bodies, our bones

carried on the inside, nothing we can discard or live
without until we determine what can be synthesized,

not necessarily disembodied, like the snail from shell,
but translated (H+) or becoming what comes next, not

just body, but uploaded, exocortex. Perhaps the artifact
we will leave is what we choose to collectively believe

into being, using sound and light, what washes over us
washes through us, stars, like shells of the sea, strung

and rung like music plucked from convergences bright,
more right than might, and all of us alone and singing.

Argonautica (call & response)

We cannot *not* know except by ignoring what's been
left behind,   and those who love the words,
the myths, wish, while we create our own artifacts,
to understand
while scholars muse and theorize.
Here from the confluence, accretion, and accrual—
        (Wikipedia)—
the golden fleece represents:

1. royal power. *Do we all want that?*
2. the flayed skin of a Greek Titan. *What would that prove?*
3. a book on alchemy. *Power in what can be transformed.*
4. a technique of writing in gold on parchment. *Elevates the word made real.*
5. a form of sift mining, a sheep fleece as strainer. *Gold in the hand is worth rock in the sea.*
6. the forgiveness of God. *The power to forgive oneself.*
7. a rain cloud. *Rain helps crops grow.*
8. a land of golden grain. *Grain satiates hunger.*
9. the hero. *The journey is the hero.*
10. the sea reflecting the sun. *Light is a power not yet wielded.*
11. the gilded prow of a sea-worthy boat. *The power to go and not be kept.*
12. a breed of sheep in ancient Georgia. *Milk, wool, meat, solace, and company.*
13. the riches brought home by explorers. *What can be found when one leaves home.*
14. the wealth or technology that can be brought home from other places. *How home can be changed when one comes back.*

15. a cult image of Zeus in the form of a ram. *Testosterone is a false high.*

16. sea silk. *Fabric made of the byssus fibers from the pen mollusk.*

17. a voyage to the Americas. *What's far and can be found and claimed.*

18. fleece dyed Murex-purple for Georgian gold. *Early economics.*

The Dark Lake by the Sea

At the foamy edge, I dipped the twin cups
of my hands to let some of it in to rinse the snot
of my crying, and a small rock moved and jumped
into my palm, and I saw it was not a rock,

but a small frog, golden, its sides billowing with aliveness.
It moved against the hill of me, hands nested in each other,
finding a good spot near my thumb's meat, and pulled itself
into itself,   and how could I move? The wind
was riffling the surface before me, and I stayed crouched,
the balls of my feet on wet pebbles, the lake nibbling my toes,
thighs beginning after a time to ache, arms around my knees,
with the small basket of my hands hanging at their end
with the little glowing being in it.
                    I'll ask again. How could I move?
I think I watched it maybe twenty minutes,

but my mind couldn't hold still.   Hair in my eyes,
I had to shake my skull, and look at the sun,
the clouds! Then a bird flew by, and my eyes followed it
hungrily—what motion! What possibility! When I looked
down again, the frog had gone.

How dumb these hands, insensitive. They hung now
like beautiful meat for another moment or two,
and then I rinsed them off in the brackish water
and upstretched, rising from my crouch to go home.

Love Alone

Who knows god as well as lovers in the park?
Everyone
listens. Everyone whispers. Even the rabbi pulls his beard.
Beauty
is an experience so overwhelming, we sometimes never
recover,
always wanting to see what remains veiled.
Boundaries
and distinction keep us safe, but the chthonic pulls

like a drenched suburban lawn, porous, liminal, sucking
at my sandal. Soaring in the air, I also necessarily

experience
the abyss which is only part of my own flight. Similarly,
I
can speak of hell only in relation to myself because I can
never
imagine the possible damnation of another as more
likely
than my own, but something rustles in the manicured verge,

the tulips dropping their rose-red. A man has lost his watch.
What time is left, he asks. I have no answer. *Show me*

your beauty, I want
to say. *Show me how you made this mask, the lichen, twigs,
the long tended griefs.*
What magic is there in that closed fist,
the rheumy eye,
the bag that watch must have fallen from?

The Plural of Apocalypse

Yes, there are days   when the bitter saliva predicts
the early loss of teeth. I am missing two. Ground until they split.
A student once told me I needed a tattoo
for the experience of pain.   I just grinned.
Here, it is already the apocalypse;   you know what I mean.
Here, I say hope is in an open palm   like a viral message:
maybe today you can stand.   I stand because I am not
alone.   After the revelation comes the touch:
touch the arm of the boy in the elevator because you smell his fear;
touch the old man delivering pizza   as you give him a tip;
give him that tip, and look into his bleary old eyes,
the sockets sagging from his wife's not-yet death,
but soon, so soon.   It's raining apocalypses,
and in the interstices,   we find out
how we will behave,   wither, blossom,   stand
          in the day after a year,   ten.   You
are not alone.   Your prospect gives me aspiration;
my commitment helps her trust again;   his pleasure
kindles the recollection not   of what is to come,
but of what is possible, the ways we find to go on:
this plural, this preponderance,   profusion,   variety of the living
as well as the beloveds, with us or gone;
a communion of gorgeous   sorrows,
our reenactment   of the ever-falling world;
what rains down, washes us   cleansing us
so we can try again.   We all reveal such pretty
marks.

Part III

Horses & Other Beings

Riding that Horse

The floors need waxing, the plumbing

is weeping, but when I am perched
on the balcony as the beast
below the house of me
surges and soars, I remember the wind

bringing the water out of the gutters
of my eyes, my hair unfurling
and, we go—should we go?
This steed and me? Yes, let's go.

Along the Wrack Line

The horse doesn't care what is deposited there:
        albums of families displaced by storms; marine
Styrofoam floats; telephone poles in parts, split,
        waterlogged, sorry and silent. Now, the horse
canters, missing everything, its great eye looking
        to the left over the space where dunes once were
to the street with slow cars, the other to the right
        seeing the waves coming and coming. Its feet know
how to land. My temple has descended, and the basket
        of my hips is balanced on the great bridge of beast-back.
I rock, thighs split baggage—everything I ever owned
        is in them—calves against ribs, feet so happy to simply
hang, the heels in charge, the throbbing of the horse
        heart, horse-lung thrum coming through the callouses
to make my ankles into bells. And I watch for what
        the wrack line gives up. The destructed, worn down,
pulverized. My horse bears me above it. If only my own
        spine could hold such a woman, and hold her with such
strength. What would I not be capable of then?

The Other Temple

1.

I don't think I could have climbed
these cliffs without falling, and my horse seemed—
Was I asleep? Is this possible?—to have flown over the rocks,
up and up, the sea giving way, letting go
of its hold on the shore, to this small mountain rising
like such things do against gravity, happy
in its seeming permanence, rock steadiness, like the male
having risen in his beauty out of the moist sand
of the woman—and this is how I have come to this other
temple, and the horse lets me off, and there,
looking out over the sea is an altar and on the altar is a shell
and in the shell is one pearl I put in my pocket
as I stare out over the long water giving off mist in the heating

atmosphere. What grit accrued to make this thing?
Who left it here for me to find? What gives me the right to claim it?
A cold, heavy wind is coming now. The gray
is getting thick. I'll need this small light to make my way,
I think. There's something higher,
calling from the dark. If I am afraid, can you blame me?

2.

When the flower presents itself on the mountain,
at first I think, like the pearl, it is for me, but the singing
in the petals makes me hesitate to pluck it. Instead,
I put this small, pink thing, so insignificant, nacreous

and iridescent—but really just simple calcium, the stuff

of bone—into the small bowl of flower. I am dissolving now,
like a pearl in vinegar, the blossom opening before me,
the voices choraling their many-petaled oneness.

Threshold

As he offered his arm, a spider landed on mine. Not one
of the small jelly-like ones, nor one of the large, fierce,
and fast ones, both of which I fear in my belly-mind,
but one with a thin, iridescent body, so narrow,

it seemed impossible,
and its legs were delicate as the fingers
of a Flamenco guitar player's, a young one,
hair hanging over luminous eyes, large through his glasses,
the performance lights making the blue

of them beam, the whites around them
like hardboiled egg,
that firmness, unbroken, yet yielding.   And his playing,
as if his fingers had memories of their own.

Witness

The dog was thirsty, the man could tell.
The choice: to crawl, maybe fall, along the edge again
to capture water, so the dog could drink,
not as he himself had done, by dipping face
into the gated reservoir, but from all he had, his shoe.
In the dark, as always, police possible,
maybe more so now than ever,
armed with their suspicion, poison in itself—
All I wanted to do, officer, was help the damned dog—
Just *dog*, no adjective nor expletive, danger in inflection.

Wearing Wise and Porous

The cormorants on the bridge to the island extend
their wings, necks long, heads tilted to the light,
like me with eyes closed, glasses off, on a late
summer day, not wanting to let go. I hold my arms
out too, sometimes   but lack the long, black, purple
feathers these birds have. Their stance is plaintive like old men
praying to their gods. Those feathers, though, are porous
so they can dive for fish or snakes, let water in and out;
which species and where they live mattering to how much
and what design.   Here, it is the double-crested, tufts
above the eyes when breeding, like old men's brows,
white and flicking in a wind. They look so wise.   Once,

a lone woman was found in a cave wearing a dress
made of black and green cormorant feathers. Those
who found her thought she thought she could fly,
but it was simply that she'd been alone a very long time.

Learning to Sing

The fiery steed of my tongue
is like that, a horse in my horse face,
all muscle and charging ahead. It is not
like a train terminal, the many lines
      coming, going,
        a portal to somewhere,
        a portal to return from where
        you went to where you came from.
The horse—my tongue—embodies itself in time.
It is hard to ride   let alone ride well.

Underwater Horse

All the horses listed in the racing form
were on Lasix; they were all on Lasix
the racing form listed. The drug keeps
their lungs from drowning; the horses
run in the watery air we don't see. We
run in packs we barely define; defining
ourselves is what we do. Alone, we are
never alone; together we very often are
lonely. Betting on horse races is never
a sure bet; the racing form lists facts
belying facts, drugs and wins, mud-fast
or slow; does she do well in the rain?
Does this one cope with pain? Shouts
loudest for the horse surging ahead
from behind, asserting muscle over
burdens, fire over water, thin dribble
of hope for the dead horses making book
in the last-century grandstands, waving
hands as if their lives depended upon
a win, and the porous sponge of lung.

At the Carousel: the Revolutionary Power of Love

When the tail of the horse in front of me fell off, I saw
it was made of real horse hair, embedded in a wooden dowel
inserted in the carved and painted beast. My left hand held
my child riding next to me, and my right was extended
to hold the head of the horse I rode, both of us ascending
and descending, but in opposition. Just down the road, there
is a spring near the gatehouse, and the old Russian man who
comes each day with his soft accent to fill empty Perrier bottles:

For me and my wife, he told me. *The minerals are good for digestion.*

When the ride stopped, I picked up the fallen tail and stuck
the dowel back in the old timber rump, thumping it
with the heel of my hand, then brushing down the hair,
long, so long it brushed the wooden platform underneath
us, now no longer turning, the slats buckled as if with salt air,
the blue paint curling to reveal the gray grain below.

Empathy

Horse track used to be something
now they store the boats they found
after the storm and huge tents
for people without a rentable place
all tore down spray-painted zero =
not reinhabitable nowhere to go sleep
under the big top someone jokes
a bloke from Arkansas come all
this way for the electric company
overtime the good pay another
guy come to chop the felled trees
horses used to work here a squiggle
horse was one rated unreliable
didn't know which way to go bet
your bet maybe hit good maybe
not the salt wind coming from
the Atlantic fans used to be frantic
hear the lost cheering hoofs in the mud
drumming wet and not quite wild.

Part IV

Funtown

Dollars and Cents, No Repent
(revisit the crash-symbol)

Mercy's left the baby home, wants to roam
like she always hated with no place to go.
Now anywhere is somewhere; boardwalk
feels steamy and clean though it's hot. The air
is mean, makes her chest feel full, wind whipping
her neck, stings and pecks. Boy playing drums
raps a beat, rudiments—diddle, flam, and drag.
She recalls a time what could be felt fresh, now
it's all about the flesh, baby-from, fat and pale,
eyes kohled, neck chokered, she feels like a dog
on a leash.   No change today, what can
she say? The drummer hits the crash cymbal, then
the ride; she's got her sorry pride, taps her thigh,
rolls her head, hair fly, sweating at the make up
running, so she looks as if she's crying, but she's
just sighing worrying, lying, hoping she's not dying.

Today he thinks, *She looks pretty,* hoping he
might just get lucky. Bang. Sticks on lap, Tino tips
his hat. She's gone again. *Ain't never gonna happen,
let it go, she just a ho,* but hope is cheap, something
he can keep while he walks it, talks it, bangs it on
the boards. He loves bodies of water too big to cross.

August Goes Like Gold

I watch the dolphins
making their way south each morning past Sandy Hook,
Long Branch, Asbury. A long boy from Brooklyn walks
the wrack line at high tide, wearing vintage board shorts
and a linen crop top, wind riffling his black-slicked hair.
The air kissing him blows south against his face and mine
as I watch him go. He sets up an umbrella to keep
the UVs at bay and the girls who come and sit. Boys flirt
from the water. *Come on in*, they beckon, squealing.

It's as if the green foam is whispering, *It's all alright.*

Everything glitters and sparkles; even the dull sand seems
to shimmer today.   Then the dolphins heading back
north, the direction the worst storms come from, the pod
moving slow and easy, dorsals slipping in and out.
     Time to go, I hear the long boy say. He stands,
flapping white linen covering his chest, a maritime flag
signaling to a stranded boat. He'll dance at Paradise
tonight, he tells the girls as if announcing it to us all.

The wind has shifted suddenly, so I can hardly hear.
Gold lamé shorts? Big tips? Is this what he's saying?
But the grin, wide and white, that's language I can read;
what pleasure it is to shine, especially in the everyday dark.

Fire in Funtown

          The other day,
a boardwalk merchant told me it's been the best summer
in a very long time. She sells posters, vinyl, used books,
T-shirts, and vintage clothes next door to the hot dog joint
named Grab A Wiener.   I recall when it opened
in spring, how funny it was, a bit obscene,
made the news,
and the objections from people
who said it gave the wrong impression
of where we live, who we are, like that TV show
people always ask us about.   The talk
these days is all fire,
the once-wetted wiring now giving way
beneath boards,
behind walls,
and this time how one started in a custard
store, then the wind ripping currents
along the boards.   Painted resin clown faces crumbling,
so cinematic.
All the phones around me ping as I board a train
which will churn forward along
the shoreline to cities north, rising gray and cold
in another hot day.   We were almost back
to living
as if the ocean isn't right here
next to us, slumbering, as if we might go on
better than we were, as if we are like everyone
everywhere.

Firebreak

It's a year later, the wind
blowing hot, heaving this boardwalk fire along.
It takes out twenty stores,
the rebuilt pier. To stop it, they bulldoze
a break in the boardwalk,
scooping out wood and metal, hoping the fire
won't leap.   Even
the fat governor looks flustered, shaking his head
on camera, patting
a woman sobbing, *How much does God expect
us to take?*
The firemen pump water from the bay, pouring
buckets over themselves
to cool off, too. September is still summer—
the news to my left—
and it is over 90 degrees today. I watch
TV while it burns, my AC on.   Thank god.
Tomorrow I'll go walk
what's left of those boards or else the beach, where
nothing is happening right now.

Rumor

The Jersey rain, my rain, soaks all as one
—Robert Pinsky

Mist spitting in off the ocean, and The Pony
sign reads *Temporary Grace*, a local band,
covers of rock, hip-hop, dance, and pop.
    Bruce is rumored to show.
Word is, from those who know, he's in town now
that *Wrecking Ball* is through.   All the locals
have a story:
     He sat on the mat next to me at Gold's Gym.
     My kid went to school with his. Ranny, for the rich.
     I saw him eating eggs at Edie's Luncheonette.
     Someone spotted him at Federici's pizza
     down Belmar way, *Looked like he was with a girl*
     not his wife.   People like to talk:
His wife, his food, his gym, his life.
The man must have a lot of memberships.
Let me be clear: I've never seen him.

TG has heard the rumors, too, plans to play hard,
not just covers, but originals, be discovered, forgiven
for not just entertaining, show what they can do.
    I've heard grace is a kind of mercy,
but they're not the same.   Mercy might be
     the audience not walking out
     when you've disappointed them;
     grace may be the chance you get
     but don't deserve.

Who knows what a band might do
        if they got a real shot? Or what grudge
        becomes grace, and who cares who shows
        when it's all the same rain,
        and you only have this
        one night to live forever in?

Three Rooms to Choose From

I sit at the bar in Porta and watch Mercy shift
her weight from leg to leg, lift one foot slightly off the ground,
shake it, then the other as if her high, high heels
hurt, then she weaves a little back and forth the way one soothes
a child in arms. She holds menus to her gut.
A couple walks in, asks about the music. *Three rooms to choose*
from, she says. *The DJ plays 80s, 90s, and pop.*
In the next room, it's house-techno, fist pumping. On the patio,
we got someone plays live if the music from the Pony
doesn't drown him out. Next, a group of girls comes in. Mercy
says, *Don't drink from nobody's cup.*
One asks her if Bruce has ever shown. *Not since I been here,*
she says. She wears an infinity scarf wrapped so no
cleavage shows, and her waist is still small even after the baby.
When she puts her hands on her hips, she wonders
what's happened to the bones underneath her skin. She says,
Could be tonight; never know, but you can always hope.

Grace Note and Shifts in Fate

Mercy wasn't working the night he came in.
On the patio, a kid playing solo, no covers,
his own songs. Bruce finished his salad, then
carried his beer outside to a picnic table,
elbows on the gray wood behind him, legs out,
one heel perched on the other ankle.   The singer
amped his performance. Bruce smiled.

People, oh people, they gathered behind, patio
filling up, even the bocce court, phones out,
texting, *Come now.*   When Bruce got up
and borrowed the kid's guitar, the place went quiet
and for a minute everyone breathed together.
            Bruce strummed
an upstroke, stopped, said, *When I was learning*

guitar, seems a million years ago, the more I stressed
over my strumming technique, the more "accidentals"
I had. Then I stopped worrying it, and it seemed like
I didn't hit the strings I didn't want so much no more.
Gotta place your focus. The rest flows from there.
Then he plucked the base note with his thumb,
croaked, *Billy bought a Chevy,* from "Seaside Bar Song,"
cocked the guitar neck to the kid who hiked his pants
and practically leaped over, his mouth open
with the words already. By the time Mercy got there,
they were on their fourth song, and she had to go through
the kitchen, the crowd thick in the fenced space,
and she stood behind the mesh door next to the stage.
            Through it, I saw

her blurred image, the baby on her hip, little fat hands
clapping along, just like us.   When Bruce was done,
he handed back the guitar, stepped into the opening sea
of patrons, and was gone. The singer choked, *Hot damn*,
into the mic, and started to play again, strong,
his own song.   Some people drifted
away, but most stayed and listened.   Mercy

opened the kitchen door and was caught
for a moment in a stray spotlight. Her head glowed
as if on fire; the air hung thick with ocean and salt.
She sucked in hard like a drowning girl rising
up from underwater, gasping,
ready to rescue
herself or grasp
a hand reaching
toward her.

All We Have for Ruins Are These Rudiments

The sand is coarse and brown like the town, small
rocks not yet pulverized, and the muscle shells and tiny

clams pepper the wrack line, the tide high, so some
bathers sit in the shadow of the old concrete pier ringed

with emergency fencing; it's crumbling, and some hard-
bitten vine trails the edges, piercing mortar between

exposed bricks, the greenery sympathetic and hopeful.
The ruins—rusty carousel house, once active furnace, old

and moldy arcade—are mute in the brilliant sun,
but for the sound of collapse, so distant and thin, I

can't hear it, but imagine creaking under the shore
wind. The concrete dust blows off a little each day,

white and fine, finer than the sand, and joining it;
and the child with his bucket under the debrided lip,

a parent calling him, *Away! Away! It's not safe*, stubbing
out his cigarette in a scooped hollow, using the meat

of his palm to shift sand over the small pile of butts
accrued there.   And listen, Tino is playing the drums.

It must be about four now.   Thursday, again.
It's him. I'd know that paradiddle and flam anywhere.

Ultra-Deep Field

In a class once, we met at night in a field
to see a nearly full moon through a telescope.
Some of us reacted by pulling away from it,
exclaiming it was so bright, it hurt. It made
some of us blink repeatedly, trying to get rid
of dark spots. I remember walking away
into the woods at the edge of the field, trying
to get to a dark place, how the moon still
hung in my eye, that no matter how alone
I felt, over us was a light so bright, I knew

if I were to get lost in the woods, whatever
direction I might walk in, I was bound
to find help.   Now, looking down
at the water, the waves have picked up;
a wind coming in from the east is deepening,
and the tide is rising, nearly licking the blanket
where a couple sits.   I watch:
a young man stands, holds his hand to a girl,
which she takes, and he hauls her up, pulls her

⁂

to him, and a telescope I hadn't noticed before
falls into the sand between them. I turn away

to speak to my companion. We hear the laughter
coming up from below, lifting over the droning

techno music pounding from The Empress down
the block, and I think of light traveling across

a universe, out of the past, how that proves
something I can't comprehend or explain.

The Cops Never Busted Madam Marie

From here, the glow of the candle between
them flickers shadows across clasped hands,
arms stretched before them toward the center
of the small, draped table. I can't see the fortune-
teller from here on the bench, but the face
of the person who has come to this Temple
of Knowledge on the boardwalk—big, blue eye
painted on the awning—is nodding, chin dipping,
mouth soft; do I imagine a trembling lip? The air
is bluing, and the mist dropping isn't quite rain;
all has gone hushed, even the falling waves slow
and muffled. As if everything is listening.   Not
for what might be overheard, but for   this
necessary intimacy between strangers,   how
any one of us might take a turn,   lay down
the back of our hands in the   open palms
of someone we believe has the   power
to tell us which door, room, or   road
we should choose, and   how to go on.

Notes

Part I

1. From the Light of Day Foundation's website: "The Light of Day Foundation, Inc., utilizes the power of music to raise money and awareness in its continuing battle to defeat Parkinson's disease and related illnesses such as PSP and ALS within our lifetime. The Foundation's mission is to fund research into possible cures, improved treatments and support for patients who suffer from those illnesses, their families and their caregivers to help improve their quality of life." For more information, please visit www.lightofday.org.

2. "Godstomp Glomp" In Monmouth County, NJ, where all of these poems are located, during a four year period, seven teenage boys stepped in front of the New Jersey Coastline Train, an epidemic for which no one has found a cure.

3. "Mercy Gets Her Krump On" This poem has a lot of dance and music jargon, starting with *krump*, which is also a great chest opener for any yoga readers. AC = Atlantic City, south of Asbury Park by about an hour and a half, another Jersey Shore destination and nightlife mecca for the lost or those with disposable cash.

4. There's a joke that everyone in New Jersey identifies where they live, where they are going, and where they have been by an exit off the major car artery the Garden State Parkway. It is not a joke. I lived off Exit 127 as a kid. Then spent a lot of years off Exit 148. Now I live off 109. The exit for Asbury Park is 100B. You can get off at 105 for Eatontown.

5. "God's Got Gaming Sense" When I was a kid in North Jersey, the local convenience store was 7-Eleven, famous for Slurpees. From their site: "You know it. You love it. But, did you realize JUST how many flavors there are? Your favorite drink comes in so many varieties, it's a marathon for your taste buds. But the good kind of

marathon where everything is delicious, and you don't have to train. Just stop in and choose an old favorite or check out our limited-time flavors. You can even make your own combo to your heart's desire."

When I lived in South Jersey, it was Wawa. From their site: "'Wawa' is a Native American word for the Canada Goose that was found in the Delaware Valley over 100 years ago. Our original Dairy farm was built on land located in a rural section of Pennsylvania called Wawa. That's why we use the goose on Wawa's corporate logo."

6. "Change the Game" *The Kingdom of Loathing* is a game. From their site: "The Kingdom of Loathing is a free, comical RPG, brought to you by the folks at Asymmetric Publications." And: "An Adventurer is You!" And: "The Kingdom contains hundreds of terrifying monsters."

A white Canadian drink differs from the white Russian in that the former is made with goat milk.

Free People was originally a funky store in Philly during the 70s, before Boho was corporatized. It became Urban Outfitters. And Anthropologie, and a whole bunch of other destination store/brands. Their site says: "During 2001, we realized that it was really Free People that invoked some of our favorite images, those of femininity, courage, and spirit. It was time to get back to our roots."

Hush Puppies are a shoe with a rangy history, starting in the military, then hip in the 60s, then only the very uncool would wear them, and they almost stopped being made; then sometime in the 90s, some young people found a warehouse in Brooklyn with thousands of them, and they gave them out free. Supposedly, they became chic street wear, and between fashion designers picking them up and Malcolm Gladwell writing about them in his book, *The Tipping Point,* they were all the rage in the late 90s. They are a pretty seriously well-made shoe regardless of what you think of the way they look and whether or not that story is apocryphal.

7. "Mercy: Rivet Girl Listen to—" Aggrotech, etc. are types of music evolved from postindustrial dance music. Rivet head subculture, dark, but not goth, was heightened in gender costumes, including corsets and sexualized clothes. Punk ancestry with a new aesthetic,

not romantic. Think PoMo (postmodern) meets rustic industrial. Think: we're oppressed and we know it; clap your hands.

Tommorowland is a gigantic EDM (electronic dance music) festival that's been held annually in Belgium for over a decade. One might say it is the Woodstock of the new millennium; one might say it's Woodstock on acid, but that would be very wrong indeed, nor is it Woodstock on ecstasy. Think Woodstock on technology. But what do I know? I haven't been to it. Other than virtually. It is a wonder, and also a great symbol of wealth disparity. It costs millions to put on and generates millions. Their rates were at this writing: "To Secure Your Personal Key to Happiness: $357 for Full Madness pass; $417 for Full Madness Dreamville Camping; $649 Easy Tent Camping Full Madness; $1,459 to sleep in the Dreamlodge; $1,660 for the Cabanas." Per person. After you get to Belgium. The audience is largely white. You can watch one of the aftermovies online. I especially like 2012: www.youtube.com/watch?v=UWb5Qc-fBvk

You can attend versions of Tommorowland all over the world. We are hungry for feeling, sense, sound, and movement. Raise your hands if you are, as well.

Skrillex is an EDM DJ star. DJs are the music scene artist of the moment.

Krewella is an EDM group: two sisters from the Chicago burbs; there was a third person, but they had a fight.

8. "Brainspin Me Another Wunna Those" In January 2014, home heating oil hit $3.50 a gallon. It cost us $900 a tank, and we needed three that winter.

Sometimes people need to charge their laptops and phones in public places. Sometimes people don't let them.

Monmouth Mall is also called Eatontown Mall. It's 15 minutes west of the Atlantic Ocean.

9. "Dr. Valentine Blows a Curse (YOLO)" YOLO = you only live once

10. "Jersey Shore Boards: Got a dollar, man?" There are many boardwalks along New Jersey's 127 miles of coast, but some famous

ones are: Wildwood, Atlantic City, Seaside Heights, and Asbury Park. Most of the boards in these poems are those of Asbury Park, but memory makes composites of all my shore years. Asbury has a sweet spot in my mind as I used to go there as a kid when there was still an amusement park. My family couldn't afford the rides, so we went in the off-season when they were closed. The only ride open was the carousel, a Philadelphia Toboggan Co. merry-go-round with wooden horses and sea creatures. We rode for a quarter. I live twenty minutes from it now. The carousel is long gone—another amusement park somewhere in the South bought the mechanics; the horses are supposedly in someone's basement somewhere. The building that housed it is still there: built in the 30s by the Beaux-Arts architects Whitney Warren and Charles Wetmore, it's round and green—copper patina—with haunting angel faces in the ornate windows. Today, sometimes there are performances in there. Right now, its interior walls are a graffiti artist display of eerie white people you can see through the barred metal doors. They nearly glow in the dark.

The characters in the poems are amalgams of people I have seen all my life.

Hurricane Sandy destroyed many miles of Jersey boardwalk, mostly in sections, and repairs were easy to spot these last couple of years because of the color and texture. New: blond, smooth. Old: gray, cracked, often a bit bowed, sometimes with loose nails. It costs a lot to replace boardwalk, so the towns keep what is salvageable. Seaside Heights' boardwalk—everyone knows this town because of the TV shots of the rollercoaster in the ocean after Sandy—cost over ten million to replace.

11. "Mercy Thinks: the Color of Blood in Any Century" Ai Weiwei is a dissonant Chinese installation artist, photographer, rebel, culture critic, and activist of international fame and controversy. One of his earlier artistic/critical exhibitions was a film of him smashing an historically significant Chinese vase purportedly as old as the Roman empire. You can see a vimeo here: vimeo.com/64886243

My first job was at McDonalds. If no one was looking, I would lick the lids of the gallon hot fudge cans when I had to refill the machine.

12. "Late Spring, Dignity" The Pony = The Stone Pony, just across from the boardwalk in Asbury Park, a very famous music venue. Bruce Springsteen, Jon Bon Jovi, among other Jersey musicians, got their starts there. The Pony has opened and closed a few times, but it's much beloved in the area, with a local following who grew up in it, and over time, it's gained a worldwide fan base as a music mecca. It hosts events all year long, indoors and out. It's not the only famous live music venue/landmark in Asbury: The Saint, the Wonder Bar, and Asbury Lanes are also vital clubs with legacies of The Jersey Shore Sound. Think Southside Johnny and the Asbury Jukes.

There really was a kid who played his kit across from The Pony on the boardwalk the same time, same night every week for a couple of years. I never knew his real name.

13. "In the Air, It's Fair" My second job was the midnight shift in a shore Dunkin' Donuts. I used to walk home on the boardwalk.

The DJ as techno music artist changed the ambitions of young music lovers: anyone who can buy the equipment can make music, become a star. Maybe.

14. "Holy and Crushing" Unless you lived here, you might not know that Hurricane Sandy was followed by a major freak snowstorm a week later. We were still without electricity or heat. We got about ten inches in my town.

Scholly = football scholarship

Bon hiver = Good winter, in French

Part II

1. "*Peoples Loves They Animals*" A wave of that height was documented off the Jersey shore.

Sea Bright is a very tiny barrier island north of Asbury Park. It's famous for seven private beach clubs, one of which has a $25K annual fee, and you supposedly need to know a celebrity or politician to get in. Cheaper ones are in $3-5K range to share a locker. Sea Bright has one public beach, and the rest is guarded by a fourteen-foot rock wall that's been there my whole life at least. Very controversial. The people who own houses across the street from it can see the ocean from their second floors. There is no parking, so to access those beaches, you have to either live there or join one of the clubs. Driving along this wall, you can't see the ocean at all. Repairs to the wall after Sandy were over $8.5 million.

During Hurricane Sandy, many pets were lost, some never found.

Many people were displaced (some were still displaced as I wrote this note two-and-a-half years later) from their wrecked homes. Since a lot of insurance companies paid for temporary housing, all the local rentals doubled, tripled, or quadrupled in price overnight.

Some people are still waiting for FEMA money, and Gov. Christie tosses the blame beach ball back and forth with the Feds.

2. "Out of the Blue, Who" Many things floated across the ocean after the great tsunami, including a barge-like trash heap to the Jersey Shore.

The Empress is a hotel on the south end of the boardwalk in Asbury Park famous for its gay/trans night life scene: Paradise in the winter, Tabu in the summer. Or is it the other way around? I have only been there in winter. Whatever door they let me in. It's across the street from the carousel house.

3. "Nautical Tattoo" The history is really something. I wrote this poem before I got my first tattoo. What a poser.

4. "*Shot it.   It was me.   You have to believe it.*" The Wind Mill is a famous local icon shaped like a windmill, with upstairs seating overlooking the main thoroughfare in Longbranch, but not the ocean anymore, since the high rise condos went up. You can eat great burgers and hot dogs and watch the traffic. It's a favorite at 3 am.

This was real local headline.

5. "Resistance and Surrender" A wrack line is the line of debris along the shore just above where high tide comes in. You can find all kinds of things there, human-made and otherwise.

6. "From Whence We Come, We Go" Argo and other projects are run out of Woods Hole Oceanographic Institute in Maine. You can read more about it here: www.whoi.edu/
H+ = posthuman or transhuman, a philosophic, pragmatic, and— dare I say this?—humane line of thinking you can read about here: humanityplus.org/

7. "*Argonautica* (call & response)" This plays off Jason and the Argonauts myth. And has fun with Wikipedia.

8. "Love Alone" It borrows its title and some of its ruminations from the theologian Balthasar's *Love Alone is Credible.*

Part III

1. "Underwater Horse" The Monmouth Park Racetrack is in Eatontown. They still have live races in the summer. It's a nasty business, much beloved and historical. This poem is about one of the drugs horses are given.

2. "At the Carousel: the Revolutionary Power of Love" There is a racetrack at Saratoga, NY, and a carousel, and many natural wells. People come from all over for the water, as well as for the races.
The floor of that merry-go-round was made like a boardwalk, wood-slatted and weatherworn.

3. "Empathy" The Monmouth Racetrack was used to temporarily house people whose homes were wrecked in Hurricane Sandy, then to house many out-of-state workers and volunteers who came here to help, and also to store the scores of boats washed from marinas onto dry land, train tracks, and people's lawns.

Part IV

1. "Fire in Funtown" In the year or two after Hurricane Sandy, there were a lot of fires along the shore as electrical wiring, once soaked, finally gave out.

Often when I travel for readings, people ask me about the TV show, *The Jersey Shore*. I've never watched it, but I assure them, it's nothing like the truth. Sometimes they tell me they want to visit where I live because of that show. I never know how to respond to that.

2. "Firebreak" The line "the news to my left" helps this poem shake hands with AR Ammons' poem, "Corsons Inlet," which is a real place, Corson's Inlet State Park on the southern end of Ocean City, NJ, GSP Exit 25.

3. "Rumor" The epigraph is from the title poem of Robert Pinsky's book, *Jersey Rain*. He grew up in Long Branch. I saw him speak/ perform with Bruce Springsteen at David Daniels' WAMFest one year at Fairleigh Dickinson University. One of them said that Pinsky had started out a musician but became a poet while Springsteen had started out a poet and became a musician. Sitting just six rows from two Jersey heroes, my eyes ran water the whole time. In delight. And inspiration. A re-invigoration. That, btw, is the real Jersey Shore.

People in my area really all do have a story about seeing or meeting Bruce. Most are probably true stories. I never have, though once I thought I saw him at the Rook Café at the Little Silver train station, but it was a guy named Jake, and the barista laughed at me.

4. "Three Rooms to Choose From" Porta is a bar, restaurant, and dance club across from The Stone Pony in Asbury park, with a rustic-industrial warehouse vibe. *Porta* = door, in Italian, and the décor includes many old ones. Before Porta, the site was a gay a-go-go joint where muscled men danced on tabletops in leather thongs.

5. "Grace Note and Shifts in Fate" The dialogue attributed to the character of Bruce Springsteen in this poem is probably from my reading of many interviews that have been done with him while I wrote papers for two of the Monmouth University/Southern Indiana University Glory Days Symposiums about the singer-songwriter. I don't recall where I read it, so can't cite the source, but I'm sure it's been torqued and twisted. I hope it doesn't offend.

6. "All We Have for Ruins" For Michael, Mihaela, and Fabe. We spend a lot of great time together on that beach, near those casino ruins.

7. "Ultra-Deep Field" The Hubble Telescope took thousands of pictures of a small area of space, which were composited to show us breathtaking images of the universe. I think this book is like that for me about the Jersey Shore: a composite I hope in confluence reveals something larger than the parts. This book is a more emotionally honest one than *Panic*, which includes only third person poems set on the Jersey Shore. In this book, the speaker is complicit, literally, as a character in some and pyscho-spiritually/lyrically in others. The speaker is the telescope.

The literal telescope in the poem was at the observatory at Stockton University. For decades, Professor Harold Taylor would open it to the public on Friday nights. After he died, it was closed. I don't know if it is still operating or not.

The speaker in the poem is sitting upstairs at Club Watermark on the Asbury Park Boardwalk.

8. "The Cops Never Busted Madam Marie" The title comes from Bruce Springsteen's song "4th of July, Asbury Park (Sandy)." The real line is "Did you hear the cops finally busted Madame Marie for telling fortunes better than they do?" Madame Marie was Marie Castello, and her little hut is on the north end of the boardwalk. Her granddaughter runs it now. It was repainted recently. It looks really good. I've never had my fortune told. Maybe I should.

Acknowledgments

Thanks to Pete Fairchild and to Sewanee Writers Conference, the Vermont Studio Center, the Bread Loaf Writers Conference, the Vermont College of Fine Arts Postgraduate Writers Conference, and the Great Mother New Father Conference. Thanks to Megan Cushing-Wilkinson, Tara Tomaino, Janna Silver-Smith, Peter Florek, Marc Santos, Lek Borja, Beth Bigler, Flower Conroy, Benjamin Busch, Brian Turner, Ilyse Kusnetz, June Saraceno, Alan Heathcock, Suzanne Roberts, Gayle Brandeis, Jared Michael Rypkema, BJ Ward, Paul Lisicky, Alison Luterman, Michael Waters, Mihaela Moscaliuc, Suzanne Parker, Janet MacFadyen, Ray Brunt, Timothy Liu, Sophie Cherry, Peter Murphy, Leslie McGrath, Kathleen Graber, Renée Ashley, Oliver de la Paz, Katie Rauk, Katie Riegel, R. Dwayne Betts, TJ Jarrett, Fred Marchant, Monica Hand, Alicia Ostriker, Julia Bouwsma, Stephen Dunn, Ellen Lesser, Andre Dubus III, Tony Hoagland, Michael Broek; to the community of writers and artists at the Sierra Nevada Low Residency MFA program in Creative Writing, Stockton University's Winter Poetry & Prose Getaway, and the Brookdale Community College Humanities Institute, all of which I am honored to teach in; and to all of the artists, musicians, and writers who hail from, thrive in, and/or survive living in New Jersey, especially along the shore and on and under all those miles of boardwalks; to Diane Goettel, Patricia Sprague Goettel, Angela Leroux-Lindsey, and to Lily and Kit, to whom I owe so much in the growing BLP tribe; to my family, friends, community/ies, colleagues—I love you all—and finally to the editors and publishers of the following who gave homes to poems though sometimes in earlier versions or under different titles and sometimes before I even knew they could hold their own:

AlteredScale: "The Plural of Apocalypse"
Beloit Poetry Journal: "Witness"

Casa de Cinco Hermanas, a Journal of Literature, Letters, and Landscape: "Grace Note and Shifts in Fate," "All We Have for Ruins Are These Rudiments," "Ultra-Deep Field," and "The Cops Never Busted Madam Marie"

Cura: A Literary Magazine of Art & Action: "First to Go, Last to Know"

Drunken Boat: "Glory of the Seas" and "The Depths"

Gathered: Contemporary Quaker Poets, Sundress Publications: "Holy and Crushing," "The Plural of Apocalypse," and "Change the Game"

Heavy Feather Review: "Godstomp Glomp" and "Moon Croon in Eatontown"

Mipoesias: "Threshold," and "Underwater Horse"

Mount Hope: "Mercy Gets Her Krump On..." "Change the Game," and *"Say It Isn't So, Ho"*

Plume Journal: "Mercy: Rivet Girl Listen To—"

Poets Artists Magazine: "Dollars and Cents, No Repent (revisit the crash-symbol)," "Empathy," and "Fire in Funtown"

Rappahannock Review: "Dr. Valentine Blows a Curse (YOLO)"

Solstice: A Magazine of Diverse Voices: "My Revenant" and "Love Alone"

TAB: The Journal of Poetry & Poetics: "Out of the Blue, Who"

The Baltimore Review: "Nautical Tattoo"

The Birmingham Review: "God's Got Gaming Sense: Everyone Loves a Slurpee," "Holy and Crushing," and "Brainspin Me Another Wunna Those"

The Good Men Project: "Daddy Trance" "Late Spring, Dignity," and "August Goes Like Gold"

The riverbabble: "The Other Temple" and "The Dark Lake by the Sea"

The Sierra Nevada Review: "Fire in Funtown"

The Wide Shore: A Journal of Global Women's Poetry: "At the Carousel: the Revolutionary Power of Love"

This Broken Shore: "Along the Wrack Line"

Photographer: Keith Huemiller

Laura McCullough's other books include, *Rigger Death & Hoist Another*, *Panic*, and *Speech Acts* and she is the editor of two anthologies, *A Sense of Regard: Essays on Poetry and Race* and *The Room and the World: Essays on Stephen Dunn*. Her writing has appeared in *Best American Poetry*, *Georgia Review*, *American Poetry Review*, *The Writer's Chronicle*, *Guernica*, *Pank*, and many other places. She is a Jersey girl.